I0017617

Azure: Microsoft Azure Fundamentals (AZ-900) Practice Tests

Your One-Stop Solution to Pass

the Microsoft Azure Fundamentals Certification Exam

Ronaldo Pelins

Table of Contents

Practice Test #1 Microsoft Azure Fundamentals (AZ-900)

Question 1:

True or false: You cannot have more than one Azure subscription per company

1. FALSE
2. TRUE

Correct Answer(s): 1

Explanation

You can have multiple subscriptions, as a way to separate out resources between billing units, business groups, or for any reason you wish.

See: https://docs.microsoft.com/en-us/azure/cloud-adoption-framework/decision-guides/subscriptions/

Question 2:

What is the name of Azure's hosted SQL database service?

1. Cosmos DB
2. Table Storage
3. Azure SQL Database
4. SQL Server in a VM

Correct Answer(s): 3

Explanation

SQL Database is a SQL Server compatible option in Azure, a database as a service

See: https://docs.microsoft.com/en-us/azure/sql-database/sql-database-technical-overview

Question 3:

Which feature within Azure collects all of the logs from various resources into a central dashboard, where you can run queries, view graphs, and create alerts on certain events?

1. Azure Portal Dashboard
2. Azure Security Center
3. Azure Monitor
4. Storage Account or Event Hub

Correct Answer(s): 3

Explanation

Azure Monitor - a centralized dashboard that collects all the logs, metrics and events from your resources

See: https://docs.microsoft.com/en-us/azure/azure-monitor/overview

Question 4:

Can you give someone else access to your Azure subscription without giving them your user name and password?

1. YES
2. NO

Correct Answer(s): 1

Explanation

Yes, anyone can create their own Azure account and you can give them access to your subscription with granular control as to permissions

See: https://docs.microsoft.com/en-us/azure/role-based-access-control/overview

Question 5:

What is a DDoS attack?

1. A denial of service attack that sends so much traffic to a network that it cannot respond fast enough; legitimate users become unable to use the service
2. An attempt to read the contents of a web page from another website, thereby stealing the user's private information
3. An attempt to send SQL commands to the server in a way that it will execute them against the database
4. An attempt to guess a user's password through brute force methods

Correct Answer(s): 1

Explanation

Distributed Denial of Service attacks (DDoS) -a type of attack that originates from the Internet that attempts to overwhelm a network with millions of packets of bad traffic that aims to prevent legitimate traffic from getting through

See: https://docs.microsoft.com/en-us/azure/virtual-network/ddos-protection-overview

Question 6:

What is the name of the group of services inside Azure that hosts the Apache Hadoop big data analysis tools?

1. Azure Hadoop Services
2. Azure Kubernetes Services
3. Azure Data Factory
4. HDInsight

Correct Answer(s): 4

Explanation

HDInsight is a collection of open-source Apache Hadoop tools

See: https://azure.microsoft.com/en-us/services/hdinsight/

Question 7:

Which of the following methods of deploying a virtual machine provides the highest availability SLA?

1. Two or more virtual machines across availability zones in the same region
2. A single VM
3. Two or more virtual machines in an availability set
4. Two or more virtual machines in a data center

Correct Answer(s): 1

Explanation

Availability Zones offer 99.99% availability when configured correctly.

See: https://azure.microsoft.com/en-us/support/legal/sla/virtual-machines/v1_9/

Question 8:

One of the benefits of the cloud is agility. What does that mean in the context of the cloud?

1. The ability to respond to and drive market change quickly
2. The ability to spin up new resources within minutes
3. The ability of a system to grow it's capacity easily when it reaches full capacity

4. The ability to recover from a big region-wide failure in a short amount of time

Correct Answer(s): 1

Explanation

Agility - the ability to respond to change "rapidly" based on changes to market or environment; ensuring fast time to market

See: https://docs.microsoft.com/en-us/azure/cloud-adoption-framework/strategy/business-outcomes/agility-outcomes

Question 9:

Which ways does the Azure Resource Manager model provide to deploy resources?

1. Azure Portal
2. Powershell
3. CLI
4. REST API / SDK

Correct Answer(s): All of the above

Explanation

All of those ways can be used to deploy or manage resources using ARM

See: https://docs.microsoft.com/en-us/azure/azure-resource-manager/management/overview

Question 10:

What feature of a system makes it elastic?

1. The ability to heal itself after a crash
2. The ability to withstand denial of service attacks

3. The ability to stay up (available) while updates are being made to the system
4. The ability to increase and reduce capacity based on actual demand

Correct Answer(s): 4

Explanation

Elasticity - The ability of a system to automatically grow when maximum capacity is reached, and automatically shrink to minimize waste.

See: https://azure.microsoft.com/en-us/overview/what-is-elastic-computing/

Question 11:

Which of the following Azure features is most likely to deliver the most immediate savings when it comes to reducing Azure costs?

1. Changing your storage accounts from globally redundant (GRS) to locally redundant (LRS)
2. Auto shutdown of development and QA servers over night and on weekends
3. Using Azure Reserved Instances for most of your virtual machines
4. Using Azure Policy to restrict the user of expensive VM SKUs

Correct Answer(s): 3

Explanation

Reserved Instances often offer 40% or more savings off of the price of pay-as-you-go virtual machines

See: https://docs.microsoft.com/en-us/azure/cost-management-billing/reservations/save-compute-costs-reservations

Question 12:

What type of container is used to collect log and metric data from various Azure Resources?

1. Azure Monitor account
2. Log Analytics Workspace
3. Managed Storage
4. Append Blob Storage

Correct Answer(s): 2

Explanation

Log Analytics Workspace is required to collect logs and metrics

See: https://docs.microsoft.com/en-us/azure/azure-monitor/platform/manage-access

Question 13:

What Azure tool gives you the ability to manage multiple subscriptions into nested hierarchies?

1. Resource Groups
2. RBAC
3. Azure Active Directory
4. Management Groups

Correct Answer(s): 4

Explanation

Management Groups - a hierarchy of subscriptions; can have many subscriptions, and group them, and put those groups into other groups

See: https://docs.microsoft.com/en-us/azure/governance/management-groups/overview

Question 14:

Logic apps, functions, and service fabric are all examples of what model of compute within Azure?

1. Serverless model
2. SaaS model
3. App Services Model
4. IaaS model

Correct Answer(s): 1

Explanation

The serverless model of compute removes all responsibility to selecting or even managing the server and makes Azure responsible for running your code including scaling

See: https://azure.microsoft.com/en-us/solutions/serverless/

Question 15:

Which Azure service is meant to be a security dashboard that contains all the security and threat protection in one place?

1. Azure Security Center
2. Azure Monitor
3. Azure Key Vault
4. Azure Portal Dashboard

Correct Answer(s): 1

Explanation

Azure Security Center - unified security management and threat protection; a security dashboard inside Azure Portal

See: https://azure.microsoft.com/en-us/services/security-center/

Question 16:

True or False: Azure is a public cloud, and has no private cloud offerings

1. TRUE
2. FALSE

Correct Answer(s): 2

Explanation

Some aspects of Azure are not open to the public and require a private agreement with Microsoft such as Azure Government and DoD services

See: https://azure.microsoft.com/en-us/overview/what-is-a-private-cloud/

And see: https://azure.microsoft.com/en-us/global-infrastructure/government/

And see: https://azure.microsoft.com/en-us/overview/azure-stack/

Question 17:

What types of resources are defined as "compute resources"?

1. Only Virtual Machines
2. All resources that are listed in the Azure Marketplace
3. Resources that perform some type of task that requires CPU cycles to perform the work

Correct Answer(s): 3

Explanation

Compute Services - a category of services in Azure that provides CPU cycles for rent. Virtual Machines are only one type of compute resource. The Marketplace contains many types of resources, not just compute.

See: https://azure.microsoft.com/en-us/product-categories/compute/

Question 18:

What feature within Azure will make recommendations to you about reducing cost on your account?

1. Azure Advisor
2. Azure Service Health
3. Azure Dashboard
4. Azure Security Center

Correct Answer(s): 1

Explanation

Azure Advisor analyzes your account usage and makes recommendations for you based on its set rules

See: https://docs.microsoft.com/en-us/azure/advisor/advisor-overview

Question 19:

What is Azure's preferred Identity/authentication service?

1. Facebook Connect
2. Network Security Group
3. Live Connect
4. Azure Active Directory

Correct Answer(s): 4

Explanation

Azure Active Directory (Azure AD) - Microsoft's preferred Identity as a Service solution

See: https://docs.microsoft.com/en-us/azure/active-directory/fundamentals/active-directory-whatis

Question 20:

What is the most number of virtual machines that can me managed under a single Virtual Machine Scale Set?

1. 1
2. 1000
3. 10
4. 100

Correct Answer(s): 2

Explanation

Up to 1000 virtual machines can be managed under a single VMSS

See: https://docs.microsoft.com/en-us/azure/virtual-machine-scale-sets/overview

Question 21:

Which feature of Azure Active Directory will require users to have their mobile phone in order to be able to log in?

1. Azure Information Protection (AIP)
2. Advanced Threat Protection (ATP)
3. Azure Security Center
4. Multi-Factor Authentication

Correct Answer(s): 4

Explanation

Multi-Factor Authentication (MFA) - the concept of having something additional to a "password" that is required to log in; passwords are find-able or guessable; but having your mobile phone on you to receive a phone call, text or run an app to get a code is harder for an unknown hacker to get

See: https://docs.microsoft.com/en-us/azure/active-directory/authentication/concept-mfa-howitworks

Question 22:

A virtual machine is called what type of hosting model?

1. SaaS
2. PaaS
3. IaaS

Correct Answer(s): 3

Explanation

Virtual Machines are Infrastructure as a Service (IaaS)

See: https://azure.microsoft.com/en-us/overview/what-is-iaas/

Question 23:

True or false: Formal support is not included in private preview mode.

1. TRUE
2. FALSE

Correct Answer(s): 1

Explanation

True. Preview features are not fully ready and this phase does not include formal support.

See: https://azure.microsoft.com/en-us/support/legal/preview-supplemental-terms/

Question 24:

What is Single Sign-On?

1. The ability to use an existing user id and password to sign in other applications, and not have to create/memorize a new one.
2. When you sign in to an application, it remembers who you are the next time you go there.
3. When an application outsources (federates) it's identity service to a third-party platform

Correct Answer(s): 1

Explanation

Single Sign-On - the ability to use the same user id and password to log into every application that your company has; enabled by Azure AD

See: https://docs.microsoft.com/en-us/azure/active-directory/manage-apps/what-is-single-sign-on

Question 25:

True or False: Azure still has some responsibilities to manage the hardware even in the Infrastructure as a Service model

1. TRUE
2. FALSE

Correct Answer(s): 1

Explanation

Yes, Azure still manages the hardware itself, the hypervisor and all of the physical elements behind the scenes

See: https://azure.microsoft.com/en-us/overview/what-is-iaas/

Question 26:

An IT administrator has the requirement to control access to a specific app resource using multi-factor authentication. What Azure service satisfies this requirement?

1. Azure Authentication
2. Azure Authorization
3. Azure AD
4. Azure Function

Correct Answer(s): 3

Explanation

You can use Azure AD to control access to your apps and your app resources, based on your business requirements. In addition, you can use Azure AD to require multi-factor authentication when accessing important organizational resources.

See: https://docs.microsoft.com/en-us/azure/active-directory/fundamentals/active-directory-whatis#which-features-work-in-azure-ad

Question 27:

Who is responsible for the security of the physical servers in an Azure data center?

1. I am responsible for securing the physical data centers
2. Azure is responsible for securing the physical data centers

Correct Answer(s): 2

Explanation

Azure is responsible for physical security

See: https://docs.microsoft.com/en-us/azure/security/fundamentals/physical-security

Question 28:

Azure Services can go through several phases in a Service Lifecycle. What are the three phases called?

1. Private Preview, Public Preview, and General Availability
2. Announced, Coming Soon, and Live
3. Development phase, QA phase, and Live phase
4. Preview Phase, General Availability Phase, and Unpublished

Correct Answer(s): 1

Explanation

Private Preview, Public Preview, and General Availability

Question 29:

Which Azure website tool is available for you to estimate the future costs of your Azure products and services by adding products to a shopping basket and helping you calculate the costs?

1. Azure Advisor
2. Microsoft Docs
3. Azure Pricing Calculator

Correct Answer(s): 3

Explanation

Azure Pricing Calculator lets you attempt to calculate your future bill based on resources you select and your estimates of usage

See: https://azure.microsoft.com/en-us/pricing/calculator/

Question 30:

Which European nation has it's own Azure Region that is specifically set for strict adherence to data privacy standard unlike any other region?

1. France
2. UK
3. Norway
4. Germany

Correct Answer(s): 4

Explanation

Azure Germany has a unique instance of Azure cloud that follows Germany's extra strict privacy standards and even has a data trustee

See: https://docs.microsoft.com/en-us/azure/germany/germany-welcome

Question 31:

What is the basic way of protecting an Azure Virtual Network subnet?

1. Azure DDos Standard protection
2. Network Security Group
3. Application Gateway with WAF
4. Azure Firewall

Correct Answer(s): 2

Explanation

Network Security Group (NSG) - a fairly basic set of rules that you can apply to both inbound traffic and outbound traffic that lets you specify what sources, destinations, and ports are allowed to travel through from outside the virtual network to inside the virtual network

See: https://docs.microsoft.com/en-us/azure/virtual-network/security-overview

Question 32:

What is the default amount of credits that you are given when you first create an Azure Free account?

1. Azure does not give you any free credits when you create a free account
2. The default is US$200
3. You can create 1 Linux VM, 1 Windows VM, and a number of other free services for the first year.
4. You are given $50 per month, for one year towards Azure services

Correct Answer(s): 2

Explanation

There are some other benefits to a free account, but you get US$200 to spend in the first month.

See: https://azure.microsoft.com/free

Question 33:

What benefit does a Content Delivery Network (CDN) provide its users?

1. For a small fee, Azure will take over management of your virtual machine, perform OS updates and ensure it's running well
2. Allows you to store data that can be retrieved later in an extremely fast and inexpensive manner
3. Allows you to keep temporarily session information on the web visitor such as their login ID or their name
4. Allows you to reduce the traffic coming into a web server for static, unchanging files such as images, videos and PDFs

Correct Answer(s): 4

Explanation

Content Delivery Network - allows you to improve performance by removing the burden of serving static, unchanging files from the main server to a network of servers around the globe; a CDN can reduce traffic to a server by 50% or more, which means you can serve more users or serve the same users faster; SaaS

See: https://docs.microsoft.com/en-us/azure/cdn/cdn-overview

Question 34:

Who is responsible for the security of your Azure Storage account access keys?

1. I am responsible for securing the access keys
2. Azure is responsible for securing the access keys

Correct Answer(s): 1

Explanation

Customers are responsible to secure the access keys they are given and regenerate them if they are exposed.

See: https://docs.microsoft.com/en-us/azure/storage/common/storage-account-keys-manage

Question 35:

Your organization has implemented an Azure Policy that restricts the type of Virtual Machine instances you can use. How can you create a VM that is blocked by the policy?

1. Use an account that has Contributor or above permissions to the resource group

18

2. The only way is to remove the policy, create the resource and add the policy back
3. Subscription Owners (Administrators) can create resources regardless of what the policy restricts

Correct Answer(s): 2

Explanation

You cannot perform a task that violates policy, so you have to remove the policy in order to perform the task.

See: https://docs.microsoft.com/en-us/azure/governance/policy/overview

Question 36:

What are Azure Availability Zones?

1. A folder structure in Azure in which you organize resources like databases, virtual machines, virtual networks, or almost any resource
2. Within each individual data center, certain racks of servers have been architected by Azure to have higher uptime than the others. If you place your apps onto this rack, you'll get higher uptime than if you let Azure do it.
3. This is the same as a region
4. A feature of Azure that allows you to manually specify into which data center your virtual machines are placed, which allows you to achieve higher availability than any other option.

Correct Answer(s): 4

Explanation

Availability Zones - Unique physical locations within an Azure region, made up of one or more datacenters; there is a minimum of three zones in each region; you can manually place your resources in an availability zone for highest availability

See: https://docs.microsoft.com/en-us/azure/availability-zones/az-overview

Question 37:

If you wanted to simply use Azure as an extension of your own datacenter, not primarily hosting anything there but using it for extra storage or taking advantage of some services, what hosting model is that called?

1. Private cloud
2. Hybrid Cloud
3. Public cloud

Correct Answer(s): 2

Explanation

The hybrid cloud is a mixture between private services (like your self-hosted applications) and public ones (like extra storage)

See: https://azure.microsoft.com/en-us/overview/what-is-hybrid-cloud-computing/

Question 38:

What makes a system highly available?

1. If it maintains 100% availability
2. It's not possible to make a highly available system
3. A system specifically designed to be resilient, with no single point of failures
4. Must have a minimum of two VMs

Correct Answer(s): 3

Explanation

High Availability - a system specifically designed to be resilient when some component of the system fails

See: https://docs.microsoft.com/en-us/azure/virtual-machines/windows/availability

Question 39:

What is the MAIN management tool used for managing Azure resources with a graphical user interface?

1. Azure Storage Explorer
2. PowerShell
3. Remote Desktop Protocol (RDP)
4. Azure Portal

Correct Answer(s): 4

Explanation

Azure Portal is the website used to manage your resources in Azure

See: https://docs.microsoft.com/en-us/azure/azure-portal/azure-portal-overview

Question 40:

Outlook 365 is what type of hosting model?

1. PaaS
2. IaaS
3. SaaS

Correct Answer(s): 3

Explanation

Outlook 365 is Software as a Service (SaaS).

See: https://azure.microsoft.com/en-us/overview/what-is-saas/

Question 41:

Which major cloud provider offers the most international locations for customers to provision virtual machines and other servers?

1. Microsoft Azure
2. Google Cloud Platform
3. Amazon AWS

Correct Answer(s): 1

Explanation

Azure has the most regions of any major cloud provider - 58 global regions.

See: https://azure.microsoft.com/en-us/global-infrastructure/regions/

Question 42:

Which tool within Azure helps you to track your compliance with various international standards and government laws?

1. Azure Government Services
2. Service Trust Portal
3. Compliance Manager
4. Microsoft Privacy Statement

Correct Answer(s): 3

Explanation

Compliance Manager will track your own compliance with various standards and laws.

See: https://techcommunity.microsoft.com/t5/security-privacy-and-compliance/announcing-compliance-manager-general-availability/ba-p/161922

Question 43:

True or false: there are no service level guarantees (SLA) when a service is in General Availability (GA)

1. FALSE
2. TRUE

Correct Answer(s): 1

Explanation

False, most Azure GA services do have service level agreements

See: https://azure.microsoft.com/en-ca/support/legal/sla/

Question 44:

What service does Azure provide as an optional upgrade to protect against DDoS attacks?

1. Azure protects against DDoS as part of it's basic offering and there is no service you can upgrade to
2. Azure DDoS Protection Standard
3. Azure DDoS Protection Basic
4. Advanced Threat Protection (ATP)

Correct Answer(s): 2

Explanation

Azure DDoS Protection Standard

See: https://docs.microsoft.com/en-us/azure/virtual-network/ddos-protection-overview

Question 45:

Which of the following is something that Azure Cognitive Services API can currently do?

1. Speak text in an extremely realistic way
2. All of these! Azure can do it all!
3. Recognize text in an image
4. Recognize faces in a picture
5. Create text from audio
6. Translate text from one language to another

Correct Answer(s): 2

Explanation

Azure can do all of them, of course.

See: https://docs.microsoft.com/en-us/azure/cognitive-services/welcome

Question 46:

True or false: you can create your own policies if built-in Azure Policy is not sufficient to your needs

1. TRUE
2. FALSE

Correct Answer(s): 1

Explanation

True, you can create custom policies using JSON

See: https://docs.microsoft.com/en-us/azure/governance/policy/tutorials/create-custom-policy-definition

Question 47:

Why would someone prefer a Consumption-based pricing model as opposed to a Time-based pricing model?

1. You can easily predict the cost of the service into the future
2. It is always cheaper to pay for consumption than to pay by the hour
3. The pricing model is simpler and easier to understand
4. You can save a lot of money if you don't use the resource often as opposed to having it available for use 24/7

Correct Answer(s): 4

Explanation

Consumption-Based Model - paying for something based on how much you used, as opposed to paying for something no matter if you use it or not.

See: https://docs.microsoft.com/en-us/azure/azure-functions/functions-consumption-costs

Question 48:

What hardware device is required to exist or be installed on your company network in order to set up a site-to-site VPN?

1. Application Gateway
2. VPN Gateway
3. Virtual machine

4. Virtual Network

Correct Answer(s): 2

Explanation

A VPN Gateway needs to be configured to connect to Azure for a private network to be established

See: https://docs.microsoft.com/en-us/azure/vpn-gateway/vpn-gateway-howto-site-to-site-resource-manager-portal

Question 49:

Which of the following is a feature of the cool access tier for Azure Storage?

1. Much cheaper to store your files than the hot access tier
2. Most expensive option when it comes to bandwidth cost to access your files
3. Cheapest option when it comes to bandwidth costs to access your files
4. Significant delays in accessing your data, up to several hours

Correct Answer(s): 1

Explanation

Cool access tier offers cost savings when you expect to store your files and not need to access them often

See: https://docs.microsoft.com/en-us/azure/storage/blobs/storage-blob-storage-tiers?tabs=azure-portal

Question 50:

Where is Azure's region in Africa located?

1. South Africa

2. Egypt
3. Cameroon
4. Nigeria

Correct Answer(s): 1

Explanation

Azure's only African data centers are located in South Africa

See: https://azure.microsoft.com/en-us/global-infrastructure/southafrica/

☐

Practice Test #2 Microsoft Azure Fundamentals (AZ-900)

Question 1:

Where do you go within the Azure Portal to find all of the third-party virtual machine and other offers?

1. Choose an image when creating a VM
2. Azure mobile app
3. Bing
4. Azure Marketplace

Correct Answer(s): 4

Explanation

Azure Marketplace contains thousands of services you can rent within the cloud

For more info: https://azuremarketplace.microsoft.com/en-us

Question 2:

What would be a good reason to have multiple Azure subscriptions?

1. There is one person/credit card paying for resources, and only one person who logs into Azure to manage the resources, but you want to be able to know which resources are used for which client project.
2. There is one person/credit card paying for resources, but many people who have accounts in Azure, and you need to separate out resources between clients so that there is absolutely no chance of resources being exposed between them.

Correct Answer(s): 2

Explanation

Having multiple subscriptions can technically be done for any reason, but it only makes sense if you have to separate billing directly, or have actual clients logging into the Portal to manage their resources.

For more info: https://docs.microsoft.com/en-us/microsoft-365/enterprise/subscriptions-licenses-accounts-and-tenants-for-microsoft-cloud-offerings?view=o365-worldwide

Question 3:

What is the maximum amount of Azure Storage space a single subscription can store?

1. 500 GB
2. Virtually unlimited
3. 2 TB
4. 5 PB

Correct Answer(s): 2

Explanation

A single Azure subscription can have up to 250 storage accounts per region, and each storage account can store up to 5 Petabytes. That is 31 million Terabytes. This is probably 15-20 times what Google, Amazon, Microsoft and Facebook use combined. That's a lot.

For more info: https://docs.microsoft.com/en-us/azure/azure-resource-manager/management/azure-subscription-service-limits#storage-limits

Question 4:

Which of the following elements is considered part of the "perimeter" layer of security?

1. Locks on the data center doors
2. Use a firewall
3. Separate servers into distinct subnets by role
4. Keep operating systems up to date with patches

Correct Answer(s): 2

Explanation

Firewall is part of the perimeter security

For more information on the layered approach to network security: https://docs.microsoft.com/en-us/learn/modules/intro-to-security-in-azure/5-network-security

Question 5:

Select the way(s) to increase the security of a traditional user id and password system?

1. Require users to change their passwords more frequently.
2. Do not allow users to log into an application except using a company registered device.
3. Use multi-factor authentication which requires an additional device (something you have) to verify identity.
4. Require longer and more complex passwords.

Correct Answer(s): All of the above

Explanation

All of these are ways to increase the security on an account.

For more info:

https://docs.microsoft.com/en-us/azure/active-directory/authentication/concept-password-ban-bad

https://docs.microsoft.com/en-us/azure/active-directory-domain-services/password-policy

https://docs.microsoft.com/en-us/azure/active-directory/authentication/concept-sspr-policy

Question 6:

What makes estimating the cost of an unmanaged storage account difficult?

1. The cost of storage changes frequently
2. You are charged for data leaving Azure, and it's difficult to predict that
3. There is no way to predict the amount of data in the account
4. You are charged for data coming into Azure, and it's difficult to predict that

Correct Answer(s): 2

Explanation

There is a cost for egress (bandwidth out) and it's hard to estimate how many bytes will be counted leaving an Azure network

For more info: https://azure.microsoft.com/en-us/pricing/details/storage/page-blobs/

Question 7:

Why is a user id and password sometimes not enough to prove someone is who they say they are?

1. Passwords must be encrypted before being stored
2. Some people might choose the same user id and password
3. User id and password can be used by anyone such as a co-worker, ex-employee or hacker half-way around the world
4. Passwords are usually easy to forget

Correct Answer(s): 3

Explanation

The truth is that someone can find a way to get a user id and password, even guess it, and that can be used by another person.

For more information on other ways to prove self-identification such as Multi-Factor Authentication: https://docs.microsoft.com/en-us/azure/active-directory/authentication/concept-mfa-howitworks

Question 8:

What is the concept of Availability?

1. The percentage of time a system responds properly to requests, expressed as a percentage over time
2. A system that has a single point of failure
3. A system must have 100% uptime to be considered available
4. A system that can scale up and scale down depending on customer demand

Correct Answer(s): 1

Explanation

Availability - what percentage of time does a system respond properly to requests, expressed as a percentage over time

For more information on region and availability zones see: https://docs.microsoft.com/en-us/azure/availability-zones/az-overview

For more information on availability options for virtual machines see: https://docs.microsoft.com/en-us/azure/virtual-machines/availability

Question 9:

What is the minimum charge for having an Azure Account each month, even if you don't use any resources?

1. $1
2. $0
3. Negotiated with your enterprise manager
4. $200

Correct Answer(s): 2

Explanation

An Azure account can cost nothing if you don't use any resources or only use free resources

For more info: https://azure.microsoft.com/en-us/pricing/

Question 10:

True or false: Azure Cloud Shell allows access to the Bash and Powershell consoles in the Azure Portal

1. TRUE
2. FALSE

Correct Answer(s): 1

Explanation

Cloud Shell - allows access to the Bash and Powershell consoles in the Azure Portal

For more info: https://docs.microsoft.com/en-us/azure/cloud-shell/overview

Question 11:

What is a benefit of economies of scale?

1. The more you buy of something, the cheaper it is for you
2. Big companies don't need to make a profit on every sale
3. Big companies don't need to make a profit on the first product they sell you, because they will make a profit on the second
4. Prices of cloud servers and services are always going down. It'll be cheaper next year than it is this year.

Correct Answer(s): 1

Explanation

Economies of Scale - the more of an item that you buy, the cheaper it is per unit

For more info: https://docs.microsoft.com/en-us/learn/modules/principles-cloud-computing/3b-economies-of-scale

Question 12:

Which of the following is not an example of Infrastructure as a Service?

1. Azure SQL Database
2. Virtual Machine Scale Sets
3. SQL Server in a VM
4. Virtual Network
5. Virtual Machine

Correct Answer(s): 1

Explanation

With Azure SQL Database, the infrastructure is not in your control

For more info: https://docs.microsoft.com/en-us/azure/azure-sql/azure-sql-iaas-vs-paas-what-is-overview

Question 13:

What is the service level agreement for two or more Azure Virtual Machines that have been manually placed into different Availability Zones in the same region?

1. 99.99%
2. 100%
3. 99.90%
4. 99.95%

Correct Answer(s): 1

Explanation

99.99%

For more info: https://azure.microsoft.com/en-us/support/legal/sla/virtual-machines/v1_9/

Question 14:

Approximately how many regions does Azure have around the world?

1. 10
2. 40
3. 25
4. 60+

Correct Answer(s): 4

Explanation

There are 60+ Azure regions currently, in 10+ geographies

For more info: https://docs.microsoft.com/en-us/azure/availability-zones/az-region

Question 15:

What does it mean if a service is in Public Preview mode?

1. Anyone can use the service but it must not be for production use
2. The service is generally available for use, and Microsoft will provide support for it
3. You have to apply to get selected in order to use that service
4. Anyone can use the service for any reason

Correct Answer(s): 1

Explanation

Public Preview is for anyone to use, but it is not supported nor guaranteed to continue to be available

For more info: https://azure.microsoft.com/en-us/support/legal/preview-supplemental-terms/

Question 16:

Application Gateway contains what additional optional security feature over a regular Load Balancer?

1. Multi-Factor Authentication
2. Web Application Firewall (or WAF)
3. Azure AD Advanced Information Protection
4. Advanced DDoS Protection

Correct Answer(s): 2

Explanation

Application Gateways also comes with an optional Web Application Firewall (or WAF) as a security benefit

For more info: https://docs.microsoft.com/en-us/azure/web-application-firewall/ag/ag-overview

Question 17:

What is the Azure SLA for two or more Virtual Machines in an Availability Set?

1. 99.95%
2. 99.90%
3. 100%
4. 99.99%

Correct Answer(s): 1

Explanation

99.95%

For more info: https://azure.microsoft.com/en-us/support/legal/sla/virtual-machines/v1_9/

Question 18:

What does it mean if a service is in General Availability (GA) mode?

1. Anyone can use the service but it must not be for production use
2. Anyone can use the service for any reason
3. The service has now reached public preview, and Microsoft will provide support for it
4. You have to apply to get selected in order to use that service

Correct Answer(s): 2

Explanation

Anyone can use a GA service. It is fully supported and can be used for production.

For more info: https://azure.microsoft.com/en-us/support/legal/preview-supplemental-terms/

Question 19:

Which of the following cloud computing models requires the highest level of involvement in maintaining the operating system and file system by the customer?

1. PaaS
2. FaaS
3. SaaS
4. IaaS

Correct Answer(s): 4

Explanation

IaaS or Infrastructure as a service requires you to keep your OS patched, close ports, and generally protect your own server

For more info: https://azure.microsoft.com/en-us/overview/what-is-iaas/

Question 20:

Which of the following scenarios would Azure Policy be a recommended method for enforcement?

1. Require a virtual machine to always update to the latest security patches

2. Allow only one specific roles of users to have access to a resource group
3. Add an additional prompt when creating a resource without a specific tag to ask the user if they are really sure they want to continue?
4. Prevent certain Azure Virtual Machine instance types from being used in a resource group

Correct Answer(s): 4

Explanation

Azure Policy can add restrictions on storage account SKUs, virtual machine instance types, and rules relating to tagging of resources and groups. It cannot prompt a user to ask them if they are sure.

For more info: https://docs.microsoft.com/en-us/azure/governance/policy/overview

Question 21:

What is the benefit of using a command line tool like Powershell or CLI as opposed to the Azure portal?

1. Cheaper
2. Automation
3. Quicker to deploy VMs

Correct Answer(s): 2

Explanation

The real benefit is automation. Being able to write a script to do something is better than having to do it manually each time.

For more info on Azure CLI: https://docs.microsoft.com/en-us/cli/azure/what-is-azure-cli?view=azure-cli-latest

For more info on Azure Powershell: https://docs.microsoft.com/en-us/powershell/azure/?view=azps-4.5.0

Question 22:

Why is Azure App Services considered Platform as a Service?

1. Azure App Services is not PaaS, it's Software as a Service.
2. You are responsible for keeping the operating system up to date with the latest patches
3. You can decide on what type of virtual machine it runs - A-series, or D-series, or even H-series
4. You give Azure the code and configuration, and you have no access to the underlying hardware

Correct Answer(s): 4

Explanation

You give Azure the code and configuration, and you have no access to the underlying hardware

For more info: https://docs.microsoft.com/en-us/azure/app-service/overview

Question 23:

Which Azure service is the recommended Identity-as-a-Service offering inside Azure?

1. Azure Active Directory (AD)
2. Azure Portal
3. Azure Front Door
4. Identity and Access Management (IAM)

Correct Answer(s): 1

Explanation

Azure AD is the identity service designed for web protocols, that you can use for your applications.

For more info: https://docs.microsoft.com/en-us/azure/active-directory/fundamentals/active-directory-whatis

Question 24:

Which tool within Azure is comprised of : Azure Status, Service Health and Resource Health?

1. Azure Advisor
2. Azure Dashboard
3. Azure Monitor
4. Azure Service Health

Correct Answer(s): 4

Explanation

Azure Service Health - lets you know about any Azure-related service issues including region-wide downtime

For more info: https://docs.microsoft.com/en-us/azure/service-health/

Question 25:

Each person has their own user id and password to log into Azure. But how many subscriptions can a single account be associated with?

1. 250 per region
2. One
3. 10
4. No limit

Correct Answer(s): 4

Explanation

There is not a limit to the number of subscriptions a single user can be included on.

For more info: https://docs.microsoft.com/en-us/azure/azure-resource-manager/management/azure-subscription-service-limits

Question 26:

What Azure product allows you to autoscale virtual machines from 1 to 1000 instances, and also provides load balancing services built in?

1. Azure Virtual Machines
2. Virtual Machine Scale Sets
3. Azure App Services
4. Application Gateway

Correct Answer(s): 2

Explanation

Virtual Machine Scale Sets - these are a set of identical virtual machines (from 1 to 1000 instances) that are designed to auto-scale up and down based on user demand; IaaS

For more info: https://azure.microsoft.com/en-us/services/virtual-machine-scale-sets/

Question 27:

What does ARM stand for in Azure?

1. Availability, Reliability, Maintainability
2. Account Resource Manager
3. Advanced RISC Machine

4. Azure Resource Manager

Correct Answer(s): 4

Explanation

Azure Resource Manager (ARM) - this is the common resource deployment model that underlies all resource creation or modification; no matter whether you use the portal, powershell or the SDK, the Azure Resource Manager takes those commands and executes them

For more info: https://docs.microsoft.com/en-us/azure/azure-resource-manager/management/overview

Question 28:

What types of files can a Content Delivery Network speed up the delivery of?

1. JavaScript files
2. Videos
3. Images
4. PDFs

Correct Answer(s): All of the above

Explanation

All of them. Any static file that doesn't change.

For more info: https://docs.microsoft.com/en-us/azure/cdn/cdn-overview

Question 29:

What database service is specifically designed to be extremely fast in responding to requests for small amounts of data (called low latency)?

1. SQL Database
2. Cosmos DB

3. SQL Server in a VM
4. SQL Data Warehouse

Correct Answer(s): 2

Explanation

Cosmos DB - extremely low latency (fast) storage designed for smaller pieces of data quickly; SaaS

For more info: https://docs.microsoft.com/en-us/azure/cosmos-db/

Question 30:

In what way does Multi-Factor Authentication increase the security of a user account?

1. It requires users to provide a fingerprint or other biometric identification.
2. It requires users to be approved before they can log in for the first time.
3. It doesn't. Multi-Factor Authentication is more about access and authentication than account security.
4. It requires the user to possess something like their phone to read an SMS or use a mobile app.

Correct Answer(s): 4

Explanation

MFA requires that the user have access to their mobile phone for using SMS or an app.

For more info: https://docs.microsoft.com/en-us/azure/active-directory/authentication/concept-mfa-howitworks

Question 31:

Which free Azure security service checks all traffic travelling over a subnet against a set of rules before allowing it in, or out.

1. Network Security Group
2. Azure Firewall
3. Advanced Threat Protection (ARP)
4. Azure DDoS Protection

Correct Answer(s): 1

Explanation

Network Security Group (NSG) - a fairly basic set of rules that you can apply to both inbound traffic and outbound traffic that lets you specify what sources, destinations and ports are allowed to travel through from outside the virtual network to inside the virtual network

For more info: https://docs.microsoft.com/en-us/azure/virtual-network/security-overview

Question 32:

Select all features part of Azure AD?

1. Device Management
2. Custom banned password list
3. Log Alert Rule
4. Single sign-on
5. Smart lockout

Correct Answer(s): 1, 2, 4, and 5

Explanation

The Log Alert Rule is not a feature of Azure AD.

See: https://docs.microsoft.com/en-us/azure/active-directory/fundamentals/active-directory-whatis#which-features-work-in-azure-ad

Question 33:

True or false: Azure charges for bandwidth used "inbound" to Azure

1. TRUE
2. FALSE

Correct Answer(s): 2

Explanation

Ingress bandwidth is free. You pay for egress (outbound).

For more info: https://azure.microsoft.com/en-us/pricing/details/bandwidth/

Question 34:

What is the concept of paired regions?

1. Each region in the world has at least one other region in which is shares an extremely high speed connection, and where there is coordinated action by Azure not to do anything that will bring them both down at the same time.
2. When you deploy your code to one region of the world, it is automatically deployed to the paired region as an emergency backup.
3. Azure employees in those regions sometimes go on picnics together.
4. Each region of the world has one other region, usually in a completely separate country and geography, where it makes the most sense to place your backups. Like East US 2 is paired with South Korea.

Correct Answer(s): 1

Explanation

Paired regions are usually in the same geo (not always) but are the most logical place to store backups because they have a high speed connection and Azure staggers the service updates to those regions.

For more info: https://docs.microsoft.com/en-us/azure/best-practices-availability-paired-regions

Question 35:

Which of the following is not a feature of Azure Functions?

1. Can possibly cost you nothing as there is a generous free tier
2. Can edit the code right in the Azure Portal using a code editor
3. Designed for backend batch applications that are continuously running
4. Can trigger the function based off of Azure events such as a new file being saved to a storage account blob container

Correct Answer(s): 3

Explanation

Functions are designed for short pieces of code that start and end quickly.

For more info: https://docs.microsoft.com/en-us/azure/azure-functions/

Question 36:

Windows servers use "remote desktop protocol" (RDP) in order for administrators to get access to manage the server. Linux servers use SSH. What is the recommendation for ensuring the security of these protocols?

1. Do not enable SSH access for Linux servers

2. Disable RDP access using the Windows Services control panel admin tool
3. Ensure strong passwords on your Windows admin accounts
4. Do not allow public Internet access over the RDP and SSH ports directly to the server. Instead use a secure server like Bastion to control access to the servers behind.

Correct Answer(s): 4

Explanation

You need to either control access to the RDP and SSH ports to a very specific range of IPs, enable the ports only when you are using it, or use a Bastion server/jump box to protect those servers.

For more info: https://docs.microsoft.com/en-us/azure/bastion/bastion-overview

Question 37:

Which of the following is considered a downside to using Capital Expenditure (CapEx)?

1. You are not guaranteed to make a profit
2. You must wait over a period of years to depreciate that investment on your taxes
3. You can deduct expenses as they occur
4. It does not require a lot of up front money

Correct Answer(s): 2

Explanation

One of the downsides of CapEx is that the money invested cannot be deducted immediately from your taxes

For more info: https://docs.microsoft.com/en-us/learn/modules/principles-cloud-computing/3c-capex-vs-opex

Question 38:

Which of the following is a good example of a Hybrid cloud?

1. A server runs in your own environment, but places files in the cloud so that it can extend the amount of storage it has access to.
2. Your code is a mobile app that runs on iOS and Android phones, but it uses a database in the cloud.
3. Your users are inside your corporate network but your applications and data are in the cloud.
4. Technology that allows you to grow living tissue on top of an exoskeleton, making Terminators impossible to spot among humans.

Correct Answer(s): 1

Explanation

Hybrid Cloud - A mixture between your own private networks and servers, and using the public cloud for some things. Typically used to take advantage of the unlimited, inexpensive growth benefits of the public cloud.

For more info: https://azure.microsoft.com/en-us/overview/what-is-hybrid-cloud-computing/

Question 39:

What is the concept of Big Data?

1. A set of Azure services that allow you to use execute code in the cloud but don't require (or even allow) you to manage the underlying server
2. A small sensor or other device that constantly sends it's status and other data to the cloud

3. An extremely large set of data that you want to ingest and do analysis on; traditional software like SQL Server cannot handle Big Data as efficiently as specialized products
4. A form of artificial intelligence (AI) that allows systems to automatically learn and improve from experience without being explicitly programmed.

Correct Answer(s): 3

Explanation

Big Data - a set of open source (Apache Hadoop) products that can do analysis on millions and billions of rows of data; current tools like SQL Server are not good for this scale

For more info: https://docs.microsoft.com/en-us/azure/architecture/guide/architecture-styles/big-data

Question 40:

In which US state is the East US 2 region?

1. Iowa
2. California
3. Virginia
4. Texas

Correct Answer(s): 3

Explanation

East US 2 is in the Eastern state of Virginia, close to Washington DC

For more info: https://azure.microsoft.com/en-us/global-infrastructure/data-residency/

Question 41:

How many regions does Azure have in Brazil?

1. 4
2. 0
3. 1
4. 2

Correct Answer(s): 4

Explanation

There are now 2 regions in Brazil.

For more info: https://azure.microsoft.com/en-us/global-infrastructure/geographies/

Question 42:

What is the concept of being able to get your applications and data running in another environment quickly?

1. Azure Blueprint
2. Azure Devops
3. Reproducible deployments
4. Business Continuity / Disaster Recovery (BC/DR)

Correct Answer(s): 4

Explanation

Disaster Recovery - the ability to recover from a big failure within an acceptable period of time, with an acceptable amount of data lost

For more info on Backup and Disaster Recovery: https://azure.microsoft.com/en-us/solutions/backup-and-disaster-recovery/

For more info on Azure's built-in disaster recovery as a service (DRaaS): https://azure.microsoft.com/en-us/services/site-recovery/

Question 43:

Besides Azure Service Health, where else can you find out any issues that affect the Azure global network that affect you?

1. Each Virtual Machine has a Resource Health blade
2. Azure Updates Blog
3. Azure will email you
4. Install the Azure app on your phone

Correct Answer(s): 1

Explanation

Each Virtual Machine has a Resource Health blade

For more info: https://docs.microsoft.com/en-us/azure/service-health/resource-health-overview

Question 44:

What is the benefit of using Powershell over CLI?

1. Cheaper
2. No benefit, it's the same
3. Quicker to deploy VMs
4. More powerful commands

Correct Answer(s): 2

Explanation

There is no benefit, only a matter of personal choice.

For more info on Azure CLI: https://docs.microsoft.com/en-us/cli/azure/what-is-azure-cli?view=azure-cli-latest

For more info on Azure Powershell: https://docs.microsoft.com/en-us/powershell/azure/?view=azps-4.5.0

Question 45:

If you are a US federal, state, local, or tribal government entities and their solution providers, which Azure option should you be looking to register for?

1. Azure Department of Defence
2. Azure is not available for government officials
3. Azure Public Portal
4. Azure Government

Correct Answer(s): 4

Explanation

Hopefully, it's clear that US Federal, State, Local and Tribal governments can use the US Government portal

For more info: https://docs.microsoft.com/en-us/azure/azure-government/documentation-government-welcome

Question 46:

Within the context of privacy and compliance, what does the acronym ISO stand for, in English?

1. Information Systems Officer
2. Intelligence and Security Office
3. International Organization for Standardization
4. Instead of

Correct Answer(s): 3

Explanation

ISO is a standards body, International Organization for Standardization

For more info: https://www.iso.org/about-us.html

Question 47:

What is the new data privacy and information protection regulation that took effect across Europe in May 2018?

1. ISO 9001:2015
2. GDPR
3. PCI DSS
4. FedRAMP

Correct Answer(s): 2

Explanation

The General Data Protection Regulation (GDPR) took effect in Europe in May 2018.

For more info: https://docs.microsoft.com/en-us/microsoft-365/compliance/gdpr?view=o365-worldwide

Question 48:

What two types of DDoS protection services does Azure provide? Select two.

1. Standard
2. Advanced
3. Basic
4. Premium

Correct Answer(s): 1, 3

Explanation

Azure DDos Protection Basic is free, while you can upgrade to Standard for a fee.

For more info: <u>https://docs.microsoft.com/en-us/azure/virtual-network/ddos-protection-overview</u>

Question 49:

What Azure resource allows you to evenly split traffic coming in and direct it to several identical virtual machines to do the work and respond to the request?

1. Virtual Network
2. Load Balancer or Application Gateway
3. Azure App Services
4. Azure Logic Apps

Correct Answer(s): 2

Explanation

This is the core feature of either a Load Balancer or Application Gateway

For more info: <u>https://docs.microsoft.com/en-us/azure/load-balancer/load-balancer-overview</u>

Question 50:

How do you get access to services in Private Preview mode?

1. You must apply to use them.
2. You cannot use private preview services.
3. You must agree to a terms of use first.
4. They are available in the marketplace. You simply use them.

Correct Answer(s): 1

Explanation

Private Preview means you must apply to use them.

For more info: https://azure.microsoft.com/en-us/support/legal/preview-supplemental-terms/

☐

Practice Test #3 Microsoft Azure Fundamentals (AZ-900)

Question 1:

What two advantages does cloud computing elasticity give to you? Pick two.

1. You can do more regular backups and you won't lose as much when that backup gets restored
2. Servers have become a commodity and Microsoft doesn't even need to even fix servers that fail within Azure.
3. You can serve users better during peak traffic periods by automatically adding more capacity.
4. You can save money.

Correct Answer(s): 3, 4

Explanation

Elasticity saves you money during slow periods (over night, over the weekend, over the summer, etc) and also allows you to handle the highest peak of traffic.

For more info: https://azure.microsoft.com/en-us/overview/what-is-elastic-computing/

Question 2:

What does the letter R in RBAC stand for?

1. Rule
2. Role
3. Review
4. Rights

Correct Answer(s): 2

Explanation

RBAC is role based access control

For more info: https://docs.microsoft.com/en-us/azure/role-based-access-control/

Question 3:

Where can you go to see what standards Microsoft is in compliance with?

1. Azure Privacy Page
2. Azure Service Health
3. Azure Security Center
4. Trust Center

Correct Answer(s): 4

Explanation

The list of standards that Azure has been certified to meet is in the Trust Center

For more info: https://www.microsoft.com/en-us/trust-center

Question 4:

True or false: Azure PowerShell scripts and Command Line Interface (CLI) scripts are entirely compatible with each other?

1. FALSE
2. TRUE

Correct Answer(s): 1

Explanation

No, PowerShell is it's own language, different than CLI

For more info: https://docs.microsoft.com/en-us/powershell/azure/?view=azps-4.5.0

Question 5:

What is the name of the open source project run by the Apache foundation that maps to the HDInsight tools within Azure?

1. Apache Jazz
2. Apache Hadoop
3. Apache Cayenne
4. Apache Jaguar

Correct Answer(s): 2

Explanation

Hadoop is open source home of the HDInsight tools

For more info: https://docs.microsoft.com/en-us/azure/hdinsight/hadoop/apache-hadoop-introduction

Question 6:

What advantage does an Application Gateway have over a Load Balancer?

1. Application Gateway can be scaled so that two, three or more instances of the gateway can support your application.
2. Application gateway understands the HTTP protocol and can interpret the URL and make decisions based on the URL.
3. Application Gateway is more like an enterprise-grade product. You should not use a load balancer in production.

Correct Answer(s): 2

Explanation

Application gateway can make load balancing decisions based on the URL path, while a load balancer can't.

For more info: https://docs.microsoft.com/en-us/azure/application-gateway/overview

Question 7:

Which two features does Virtual Machine Scale Sets provide as part of the core product? Pick two.

1. Firewall
2. Autoscaling of virtual machines
3. Automatic installation of supporting apps and deployment of custom code
4. Load balancing between virtual machines
5. Content Delivery Network

Correct Answer(s): 2, 4

Explanation

VMSS provides autoscale features and has a built in load balancer. You still need to have a way to deploy your code to the new servers, as you do with regular VMs.

For more info: https://docs.microsoft.com/en-us/azure/virtual-machine-scale-sets/

Question 8:

Which tool within the Azure Portal will make specific recommendations based on your actual usage for how you can improve your use of Azure?

1. Azure Advisor
2. Azure Monitor
3. Azure Dashboard
4. Azure Service Health

Correct Answer(s): 1

Explanation

Azure Advisor - a tool that will analyze your use of Azure and make you specific recommendations based on your usage across availability, security, performance and cost categories

For more info: https://docs.microsoft.com/en-us/azure/advisor/

Question 9:

TRUE OR FALSE: Through Azure Active Directory one can control access to an application but not the resources of the application.

1. TRUE
2. FALSE

Correct Answer(s): 2

Explanation

Azure AD can control the access of both the apps and the app resources.

See: https://docs.microsoft.com/en-us/azure/active-directory/fundamentals/active-directory-whatis#which-features-work-in-azure-ad

Question 10:

With Azure public cloud, anyone with a valid credit card can sign up and get services immediately

1. FALSE
2. TRUE

Correct Answer(s): 2

Explanation

Yes, Azure public cloud is open to the public in all countries that Azure supports.

For more info: https://docs.microsoft.com/en-us/learn/modules/create-an-azure-account/

Question 11:

What software is used to synchronize your on premises AD with your Azure AD?

1. Azure AD Domain Services
2. AD Connect
3. LDAP
4. Azure AD Federation Services

Correct Answer(s): 2

Explanation

AD Connect is used to synchronize your corporate AD with Azure AD.

For more info: https://docs.microsoft.com/en-us/azure/active-directory/hybrid/whatis-azure-ad-connect

Question 12:

What is the recommended way within Azure to store secrets such as private cryptographic keys?

1. Azure Key Vault

2. In an Azure Storage account private blob container
3. Azure Advanced Threat Protection (ATP)
4. Within the application code

Correct Answer(s): 1

Explanation

Azure Key Vault - the modern way to store cryptographic keys, signed certificates and secrets in Azure

For more info: https://docs.microsoft.com/en-us/azure/key-vault/

Question 13:

What is the significance of the Azure region? Why is it important?

1. Region is just a folder structure in which you organize resources, much like file folders on a computer.
2. Once you select a region, you cannot create resources outside of that region. So selecting the right region is an important decision.
3. Even though you have to choose a region when creating resources, there's generally no consequence of what you select. You can create a network in one region and then create virtual machines for that network in another region.
4. You must select a region when creating most resources, and the region is the area of the world where those resources will be physically located.

Correct Answer(s): 4

Explanation

The region is the area of the world where resources get created. You can create resources in any region that you have access to. But there are sometimes restrictions when creating a resource in one region that related resources like networks must also be in the same region for logical reasons.

For more info: https://azure.microsoft.com/en-us/global-infrastructure/geographies/#overview

Question 14:

How many minutes per month downtime is 99.99% availability?

1. 1
2. 4
3. 40
4. 100

Correct Answer(s): 2

Explanation

99.99% is 4 minutes per month of downtime

For more info: https://azure.microsoft.com/en-us/support/legal/sla/summary/

Question 15:

True or false: If your feature is in the General Availability phase, then your feature will receive support from all Microsoft support channels.

1. TRUE
2. FALSE

Correct Answer(s): 1

Explanation

This is true. Do not use preview features in production apps.

For more info: https://azure.microsoft.com/en-us/support/legal/preview-supplemental-terms/

Question 16:

Which of the following elements is considered part of the "network" layer of network security?

1. Keep operating systems up to date with patches
2. Locks on the data center doors
3. Use a firewall
4. Separate servers into distinct subnets by role

Correct Answer(s): 4

Explanation

Subnets is part of network security

For more info: https://docs.microsoft.com/en-us/azure/security/fundamentals/network-best-practices

and

https://en.wikipedia.org/wiki/OSI_model

Question 17:

Which feature within Azure alerts you to service issues that happen in Azure itself, not specifically related to your own resources?

1. Azure Monitor
2. Azure Security Center
3. Azure Portal Dashboard
4. Azure Service Health

Correct Answer(s): 4

Explanation

Azure Service Health - lets you know about any Azure-related service issues including region-wide downtime

For more info: https://docs.microsoft.com/en-us/azure/service-health/

Question 18:

TRUE OR FALSE: If you wanted to deploy a virtual machine to China, you would just choose the China region from the drop down.

1. TRUE
2. FALSE

Correct Answer(s): 2

Explanation

Some regions of the world require special contracts with the local provider such as Germany and China.

For more info: https://docs.microsoft.com/en-us/azure/china/overview-checklist

Question 19:

What are resource groups?

1. Based on the tag assigned to a resource by the deployment script, it is assigned to a group
2. A folder structure in Azure in which you organize resources like databases, virtual machines, virtual networks, or almost any resource
3. Automatically assigned groups of resources that all have the same type (virtual machine, app service, etc)

4. Within Azure security model, users are organized into groups, and those groups are granted permissions to resources

Correct Answer(s): 2

Explanation

Resource Groups - a folder structure in Azure in which you organize resources like databases, virtual machines, virtual networks, or almost any resource

For more info: https://docs.microsoft.com/en-us/azure/azure-resource-manager/management/manage-resource-groups-portal

Question 20:

What does it mean that security is a "shared model" in Azure?

1. Azure takes no responsibility for security.
2. Both users and Azure have responsibilities for security.
3. You must keep your security keys private and ensure it doesn't get out.
4. Azure takes care of security completely.

Correct Answer(s): 2

Explanation

The shared security model means that, depending on the application model, you and Azure both have roles in ensuring a secure environment.

For more info: https://docs.microsoft.com/en-us/azure/security/fundamentals/shared-responsibility

Question 21:

Which of the following would be an example of an Internet of Things (IoT) device?

1. A refrigerator that monitors how much milk you have left and sends you a text message when you are running low
2. A web application that people use to perform their banking tasks
3. A video game, installed on Windows clients around the world, that keep user scores in the cloud.
4. A mobile application that is used to watch online video courses

Correct Answer(s): 1

Explanation

An IoT device is not a standard computing device but connects to a network to report data on a regular basis. A web server, a personal computer, or a mobile app is not an IoT device.

For more info: https://docs.microsoft.com/en-us/azure/iot-fundamentals/iot-introduction

Question 22:

What type of documents does the Microsoft Service Trust Portal provide?

1. A list of standards that Microsoft follows, pen test results, security assessments, white papers, faqs, and other documents that can be used to show Microsoft's compliance efforts
2. A tool that helps you manage your compliance to various standards
3. Specific recommendations about your usage of Azure and ways you can improve
4. Documentation on the individual Azure services and solutions

Correct Answer(s): 1

Explanation

A list of standards that Microsoft follows, pen test results, security assessments, white papers, faqs, and other documents that can be used to show Microsoft's compliance efforts

For more info: https://servicetrust.microsoft.com/

Question 23:

What are groups of subscriptions called?

1. ARM Groups
2. Subscription Groups
3. Management Groups
4. Azure Policy

Correct Answer(s): 3

Explanation

Subscriptions can be nested and placed into management groups to make managing them easier.

For more info: https://docs.microsoft.com/en-us/azure/governance/management-groups/overview

Question 24:

Which Azure service can be enabled to enable Multi-Factor Authentication for administrators but not require it for regular users?

1. Advanced Threat Protection
2. Azure Firewall
3. Privileged Identity Management
4. Azure AD B2B

Correct Answer(s): 3

Explanation

Privileged Identity Management can be used to ensure privileged users have to jump through additional verification because of their role.

For more info: https://docs.microsoft.com/en-us/azure/active-directory/privileged-identity-management/pim-configure

Question 25:

How does Multi-Factor Authentication make a system more secure?

1. It doesn't make it more secure
2. It allows the user to log in without a password because they have already previously been validated using a browser cookie
3. It is another password that a user has to memorize, making it more secure
4. It requires the user to have access to their verified phone in order to log in

Correct Answer(s): 4

Explanation

Multi-Factor Authentication (MFA) - the concept of having something additional to a "password" that is required to log in; passwords are find-able or guessable; but having your mobile phone on you to receive a phone call, text or run an app to get a code is harder for an unknown hacker to get

For more info: https://docs.microsoft.com/en-us/azure/active-directory/authentication/concept-mfa-howitworks

Question 26:

How many hours are available free when using the Azure B1S General Purpose Virtual Machines under a Azure free account in the first 12 months?

1. 750 hrs
2. Indefinite amount of hrs
3. 500 hrs
4. 300 hrs

Correct Answer(s): 1

Explanation

Each Azure free account includes 750 hours free for Azure B1S General Purpose Virtual Machines for the first 12 months.

For more info: https://azure.microsoft.com/en-us/free/free-account-faq/

Question 27:

What is an Azure Subscription?

1. Each user account is associated with a unique subscription. If you need more than one subscription, you need to create multiple user accounts.
2. It is the level at which services are billed. All resources created under a subscription are billed to that subscription.

Correct Answer(s): 2

Explanation

Subscription is the level at which things get billed. Multiple users can be associated with a subscription at various permission levels.

For more info: https://docs.microsoft.com/en-us/services-hub/health/azure_sponsored_subscription

Question 28:

What is the goal of a DDoS attack?

1. To extract data from a database
2. To crack the password from administrator accounts
3. To overwhelm and exhaust application resources
4. To trick users into giving up personal information

Correct Answer(s): 3

Explanation

DDoS is a type of attack that tries to exhaust application resources. The goal is to affect the application's availability and its ability to handle legitimate requests.

For more info: https://docs.microsoft.com/en-us/azure/virtual-network/ddos-protection-overview

Question 29:

What happens if Azure does not meet its own Service Level Agreement guarantee (SLA)?

1. It's not possible. Azure will always meet it's SLA?
2. You will be financially refunded a small amount of your monthly fee
3. The service will be free that month

Correct Answer(s): 2

Explanation

Microsoft offers a refund of 10% or 25% depending on how badly they miss their service guarantee

For more info: https://azure.microsoft.com/en-us/support/legal/sla/

Question 30:

If you have an Azure free account, with a $200 credit for the first month, what happens when you reach the $200 limit?

1. Your account is automatically closed.
2. You cannot create any more resources until you add more credits to the account.
3. All services are stopped and you must decide whether you want to convert to a paid account or not.
4. Your credit card is automatically billed.

Correct Answer(s): 3

Explanation

Using up the free credits causes all your resources to be stopped until you decide to get a paid account.

For more info: https://azure.microsoft.com/en-us/free/free-account-faq/

Question 31:

Which of the following services would NOT be considered Infrastructure as a Service?

1. Azure Functions App
2. Virtual Network Interface Card (NIC)
3. Virtual Network
4. Virtual Machine

Correct Answer(s): 1

Explanation

Functions are small pieces of code that you give to Azure to run for you, and you have no access to the underlying infrastructure.

For more info: https://docs.microsoft.com/en-us/azure/azure-functions/

Question 32:

For tax optimization, which type of expense is preferable?

1. OpEx
2. CapEx

Correct Answer(s): 1

Explanation

Operating Expenditure is thought to be perferable because you can fully deduct expenses when they are incurred

For more info: https://docs.microsoft.com/en-us/azure/cloud-adoption-framework/strategy/business-outcomes/fiscal-outcomes

Question 33:

Where is Azure's region in the Middle East located?

1. Jordan
2. Turkey
3. Saudi Arabia
4. UAE

Correct Answer(s): 4

Explanation

Azure's only Middle Eastern data centers are located in UAE

For more info: https://azure.microsoft.com/en-us/global-infrastructure/geographies/#overview

Question 34:

What data format are ARM templates created in?

1. JSON
2. XML
3. YAML
4. HTML

Correct Answer(s): 1

Explanation

ARM templates are created in JSON

For more info: https://docs.microsoft.com/en-us/azure/azure-resource-manager/management/overview

Question 35:

TRUE OR FALSE: Azure Tenant is a dedicated and trusted instance of Azure Active Directory that's automatically created when your organization signs up for a Microsoft cloud service subscription.

1. FALSE
2. TRUE

Correct Answer(s): 2

Explanation

Yes, Azure Tenant is a dedicated and trusted instance of Azure AD that's automatically created when your organization signs up for a Microsoft cloud service subscription.

See: https://docs.microsoft.com/en-us/azure/active-directory/fundamentals/active-directory-whatis#which-features-work-in-azure-ad

Question 36:

Which database product offers "sub 5 millisecond" response times as a feature?

1. Cosmos DB
2. SQL Server in a VM
3. SQL Data Warehouse
4. Azure SQL Database

Correct Answer(s): 1

Explanation

Cosmos DB is low latency, and even offers sub 5-ms response times at some levels.

For more info: https://docs.microsoft.com/en-us/azure/cosmos-db/introduction

Question 37:

What is a policy initiative in Azure?

1. A custom designed policy
2. Requiring all resources in Azure to use tags
3. The ability to group policies together
4. Assigning permissions to a role in Azure

Correct Answer(s): 3

Explanation

The ability to group policies together

For more info: https://docs.microsoft.com/en-us/azure/governance/policy/overview#initiative-definition

Question 38:

Which style of computing is easiest when migrating an existing hosted application from your own data center into the cloud?

1. Serverless
2. PaaS
3. FaaS
4. IaaS

Correct Answer(s): 4

Explanation

Infrastructure as a service is the easiest to migrate into, from an existing hosted app - lift and shift

For more info: https://azure.microsoft.com/en-us/overview/what-is-iaas/

Question 39:

If you wanted to get an alert every time a new virtual machine is created, where could you create that?

1. Azure Policy
2. Azure Monitor
3. Subscription settings
4. Azure Dashboard

Correct Answer(s): 2

Explanation

The best place to track events at the resource level is Azure Monitor.

For more info: https://docs.microsoft.com/en-us/azure/azure-monitor/

Question 40:

What is the core problem that you need to solve in order to have a high-availability application?

1. You need to ensure the capacity of your server exceeds your highest number of expected concurrent users
2. You need to ensure your server has a lot of RAM and a lot of CPUs
3. You should have a backup copy of your application on standby, ready to be started up when the main application fails.
4. You need to avoid single points of failure

Correct Answer(s): 4

Explanation

You'll want to avoid single points of failure, so that any component that fails does not cause the entire application to fail.

For more info: https://docs.microsoft.com/en-us/azure/architecture/guide/design-principles/redundancy

Question 41:

Which of the following resources are not considered Compute resources?

1. Function Apps
2. Load Balancer
3. Azure Batch
4. Virtual Machine Scale Sets
5. Virtual Machines

Correct Answer(s): 2

Explanation

A load balancer is a networking product, and does not execute your code.

For more info: https://docs.microsoft.com/en-us/azure/load-balancer/load-balancer-overview

For more information on compute resources: https://azure.microsoft.com/en-us/product-categories/compute/

Question 42:

Which Azure service, when enabled, will automatically block traffic to or from known malicious IP addresses and domains?

1. Azure Firewall
2. Azure Active Directory
3. Load Balancer
4. Network Security Groups

Correct Answer(s): 1

Explanation

Azure Firewall has a threat-intelligence option that will automatically block traffic to/from bad actors on the Internet.

For more info: https://docs.microsoft.com/en-us/azure/firewall/

Question 43:

What is the service level agreement for two or more Azure Virtual Machines that have been placed into the same Availability Set in the same region?

1. 99.95%
2. 99.99%
3. 100%
4. 99.90%

Correct Answer(s): 1

Explanation

99.95%

For more info: https://azure.microsoft.com/en-us/support/legal/sla/virtual-machines/v1_9/

Question 44:

What is the name of the collective set of APIs that provide machine learning and artificial intelligence services to your own applications like voice recognition, image tagging, and chat bot?

1. Natural Language Service, LUIS
2. Cognitive Services
3. Azure Batch
4. Azure Machine Learning Studio

Correct Answer(s): 2

Explanation

Azure Cognitive Services is the set of Machine Learning and AI API's

For more info: https://docs.microsoft.com/en-us/azure/cognitive-services/

Question 45:

How do you stop your Azure account from incurring costs above a certain level without your knowledge?

1. Switch to Azure Reserved Instances with Hybrid Benefit for VMs
2. Only use Azure Functions which have a significant free limit
3. Set up a billing alert to send you an email when it reaches a certain level
4. Implement the Azure spending limit in the Account Center

Correct Answer(s): 4

Explanation

If you don't want to spend over a certain amount, implement a spending limit in the account center

For more info: https://docs.microsoft.com/en-us/azure/cost-management-billing/manage/spending-limit

Question 46:

What does it mean if a service is in Private Preview mode?

1. Anyone can use the service for any reason
2. The service is generally available for use, and Microsoft will provide support for it
3. You have to apply to get selected in order to use that service
4. Anyone can use the service but it must not be for production use

Correct Answer(s): 3

Explanation

Private Preview means you have to apply to use a service, and you may or may not be selected

For more info: https://azure.microsoft.com/en-us/support/legal/preview-supplemental-terms

Question 47:

Which of the following are one of the advantages of running your cloud in a private cloud?

1. Private cloud is significantly cheaper than the public cloud.
2. Assurance that your code, data and applications are running on isolated hardware, and on an isolated network.

3. You own the hardware, so you can change private cloud hosting providers easily.

Correct Answer(s): 2

Explanation

Private cloud generally means that you are running your code on isolated computing, not mixed in with other companies.

For more info: https://azure.microsoft.com/en-us/overview/what-are-private-public-hybrid-clouds/

Question 48:

Deploying Azure App Services applications consists of what two components? Pick two.

1. Managing operating system updates
2. Configuration
3. Packaged code
4. Database scripts

Correct Answer(s): 2, 3

Explanation

Azure App Services, platform as a service, consists of code and configuration.

For more info: https://docs.microsoft.com/en-us/azure/app-service/

Question 49:

Why should you divide your application into multiple subnets as opposed to having all your web, application and database servers running on the same subnet?

1. Each server type of your application requires its own subnet. It's not possible to mix web servers, database servers and application servers on the same subnet.
2. There are only a limited number of IP addresses available per subnet, so you need multiple subnets over a certain number.
3. Separating your application into multiple subnets allows you to have different NSG security rules for each subnet, which can make it harder for a hacker to get from one compromised server onto another.

Correct Answer(s): 3

Explanation

For security purposes, you should not allow "port 80" web traffic to reach certain servers, and you do that by having separate NSG rules on each subnet.

For more info: https://docs.microsoft.com/en-us/azure/security/fundamentals/network-best-practices

Question 50:

What operating systems does an Azure Virtual Machine support?

1. Linux
2. Windows, Linux and macOS
3. macOS
4. Windows and Linux
5. Windows

Correct Answer(s): 4

Explanation

Azure Virtual Machines support Windows and Linux

For more info: https://docs.microsoft.com/en-us/azure/virtual-machines/

www.ingramcontent.com/pod-product-compliance
Lightning Source LLC
La Vergne TN
LVHW051747050326
832903LV00029B/2762